LONDON

This Beautiful City

This Beautiful City

LONDON

John Freeman and Sue Sharpe

TO THE TRAITORS' GATE

Bison Books

College of the Ouachitas

Published by
Bison Books Ltd
176 Old Brompton Road
London SW5
England

Copyright © 1986 Bison Books Ltd

ISBN 0-86124-252-1

Printed in Hong Kong

Acknowledgments

The publishers would like to thank the
following individuals and agencies for their
help in the preparation of this book:

The British Library
Brompton Oratory
Bronica UK Ltd
Harrods
Leighton House
MCC
The Royal Hospital, Chelsea
Studio Workshop Ltd
Westminster Abbey
Whitbread Brewery
Martin Bristow, the designer

Page 1: *The dragon marks the City boundary
on all the major thoroughfares.*
Pages 2–3: *Guarding the entrance to the City,
the Tower of London stands on the banks of the
River Thames.*
Pages 4–5: *The fairytale outline of Tower
Bridge against the setting sun.*

Contents

Introduction

London means different things to different people. To some it is simply home, a place to live and work in, while to others who only visit, it may mean a city of history and culture, full of museums, galleries and historic buildings. Other visitors come to view the pomp and ceremony, or take extravagant shopping sprees, or spend time sampling the theatres, cinemas, clubs and restaurants in London's West End.

For London's inhabitants, it is often all too easy to take it for granted, and travel with unseeing eyes past places that draw people far and wide, unaware of the treasure on their doorsteps. It is sometimes only through taking children round museums, for instance, that people discover how enjoyable this can be. London's art, architecture, parks, gardens, museums, palaces, and royal ceremonies are there for everyone to explore, as are its similar but lesser-known attractions found tucked away down back streets or in outlying parts of the city.

There are places of course that everyone thinks they know, and that make up the familiar sights of London. St Paul's Cathedral, for example, is passed every day by thousands of City workers, but many probably have little idea just how long a church has stood on that spot, how many times it has been rebuilt, how it was once used for stabling horses, and with

what commitment Sir Christopher Wren spent 35 years of his life supervising every part of its construction.

Another characteristic sight is the Houses of Parliament and Big Ben. The name actually refers not to the clock tower or the clock itself but to the huge 13½-ton bell that strikes the hour. It was named after Sir Benjamin Hall, Commissioner of Works, and winched into position in 1858, where it has remained ever since. Four other bells make up the chime that radio news listeners and local inhabitants alike instantly recognize. Even in this technological age, the clock is still wound by hand, and tells the precise time on its four 23-foot-wide faces. Adjoining the first floor of the clock tower is a small room in which recalcitrant Members of Parliament can be imprisoned. The last to be detained was Charles Bradlaugh, the free-thinker who refused to take the oath in 1880.

Buckingham Palace, the London residence of the Queen, needs little introduction. There is always a cluster of people waiting patiently outside when the royal family are in London. Most busy Londoners do not give it a second glance, but if by chance the traffic is held up to allow a fleet of black limousines out of the big gates, curiosity cannot be suppressed and eyes are strained for a glimpse of modern-day queens, princes and princesses. The Palace itself has more the look of a country residence, and in fact it started life as such in the early 18th Century. George III bought it from the Duke of Buckingham in 1762 for his Queen, Charlotte of Germany. Then called Buckingham House, it was soon outgrown by George's eleven children and the family moved to Windsor. It was not until 1825 that it became

Previous pages: Dawn breaks over St Paul's Cathedral and the City.
Left: Reflected in one of London's modern buildings is the telecommunications centre of the Post Office Tower.
Below: An outline plan of central London showing the major monuments.

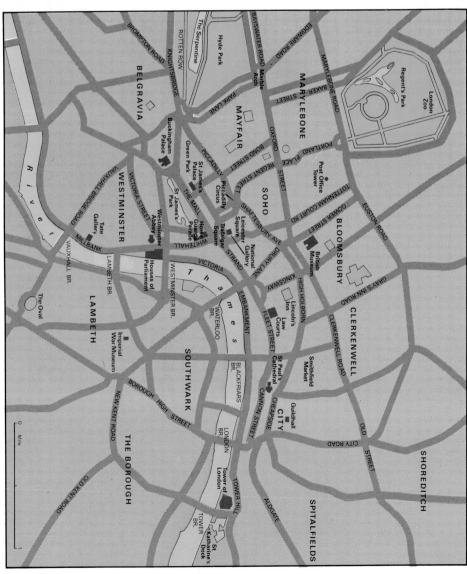

Left: Buckingham Palace, the London home of the reigning monarch since the 18th Century.
Above: Horseguards Parade, where the Queen's official birthday is celebrated with the Trooping of the Colour.
Below: After the ceremony, the Guards return to barracks in a spectacular parade down The Mall.

the Palace, after being remodelled by Nash for George IV. It is around Buckingham Palace and nearby St James's Palace that London's most colourful pageantry takes place, where the sight of the daily Changing of the Guard, or the procession of Life Guards riding down The Mall cannot fail to attract attention.

At the other end of the broad sweep of The Mall is Trafalgar Square, a favourite gathering place for both locals and visitors. Flanked by the National Gallery on one side and St Martin-in-the-Fields on another, it is usually a leisurely place where Nelson gazes down from his column to the scene below. Children feed the fat pigeons that waddle placidly about; punks with brightly coloured hair and leather jackets swing their legs on the stone edges of the fountains; marchers demonstrating for a

social or political cause end up here for rousing speeches after walking all the way from Speakers' Corner in Hyde Park; and on New Year's Eve, the square is packed with revellers singing and dancing the Old Year out and the New Year in.

While royal families may have spent many happy times at Buckingham Palace, their earlier residence, another instantly recognizable London landmark, has rather more turbulent associations. The Tower of London still presents an awesome sight, as it must have done to those unfortunates ferried across to Traitors' Gate, knowing they may never come out alive. Built by William the Conqueror to cover the river approaches to London, the Tower has served as fortress, palace and state prison. Its history as a place of murder and execution is one that leaps most readily to mind. The gruesome tales of the 'two little princes', Edward V and the Duke of York, who were smothered in the Bloody Tower, and the executions of two of Henry VIII's wives, Anne Boleyn and Catharine Howard, are just a few of the infamous incidents which took place in the Tower. The last person to be executed

there was a German spy, who was shot in 1941. It is not surprising that the place is held to be haunted. Today it attracts thousands of visitors, who line up for hours to see the Crown Jewels on display, and have their picture taken with the Yeomen Warders. The Yeomen are often mistakenly called 'beefeaters', a corruption of the French *boufitiers*, or guardians of the King's buffet. The large, black ravens have a long association with the Tower; it is believed that if they ever disappear England will fall, and that ill-fortune will befall anyone who harms them. Consequently they are very well cared for.

Any Londoner who has spent time living abroad experiences some nostalgic feelings on seeing a red London bus. The double-decker is one of London's best-known sights, and adds a broad splash of colour to grey roads and buildings. If you have time to spare, one of the most pleasant ways to see the city is from the top of a double decker bus; a number 22, for example, will take you all the way from Homerton in east London, through the City, the West End, and Chelsea to Putney in south-west London.

London's early boundaries were set by the transport available. The development of the railways in the 1800s changed society within a generation, bringing an increase in London's population and an expansion in city suburbs. At the beginning of the 19th Century, Euston Road was London's northern boundary, along which three giant termini – Euston, King's Cross and St Pancras – were built to facilitate easy entry and escape from the metropolis. During their construction, Charles Dickens was living in nearby Doughty Street, and the turmoil involved is described in his novel *Dombey and Son*. While Euston and King's Cross are quite unostentatious, the railway hotel designed by Sir Gilbert Scott fronting St Pancras Station is a fine example of Gothic revival architecture. Its pinnacled heights rise

up like a giant fairy castle, and present a vivid contrast to the surrounding functional city landscape.

Happening upon this somewhat eccentric façade may surprise the onlooker, but its size makes it a clear landmark. Smaller and lesser-known places have to be searched for. Ancient churches and historic pubs have seen a wealth

Opposite: Trafalgar Square, dominated by Nelson's Column, is a meeting place for Londoners and tourists alike.
Below: Surrounded by an ever-changing city skyline, the dome of St Paul's retains its 17th-Century grandeur.

of social history through the people they have played host to and the historic events that have occurred within and around them, such as the Plague, the Great Fire, and various rebellions and wars. Exploring back streets, discovering street markets, wandering along the canal towpath past elegant terraces or urban dilapidation all add different aspects to a personal experience of London.

Over the centuries, much of the city's historical heritage has become absorbed into the ever-widening sprawl. Hyde Park, Regent's Park and Richmond Park, once the hunting grounds of kings, are now public parks enclosed by residential housing and office blocks.

In the City, the hub of high finance, some of London's oldest buildings are dwarfed by giant office blocks. Spires and towers of old churches are only just distinguishable among square blocks of concrete and glass. The city is constantly changing shape as new buildings go up and others are demolished. While new sights appear, some familiar features are disappearing, such as the Thames Barrier, such as the old red telephone boxes, which are being replaced by modern ones painted brown and yellow. Yet steeped as it is in tradition, the essential character of London remains the same, and its various charms continue to exert a magnetic attraction.

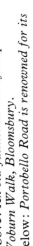

Above: An old-fashioned row of shops in Woburn Walk, Bloomsbury.
Below: Portobello Road is renowned for its antique shops and stalls, while Petticoat Lane (opposite) provides bargain-hunters with everything from socks to videos.

A Breath of Fresh Air

*A*ny busy city can become oppressive. Surrounded by concrete, brick and glass, invaded by the noise of people and traffic, there are times when everyone longs for an open grassy space, a secluded woodland walk or a view across the river. Fortunately, within the cluster of London's streets it is possible to escape to many such places, which vary from open heathland and landscaped parks and gardens to sheltered wooded glades and small leafy squares.

Viewed from above, London's green parks and gardens stand out clearly from the more sombre colours of houses and office blocks. Scattered all over the city are grassy areas of every shape and character in which to walk, run, play games, fly kites, sunbathe, read, or just sit and think in peace. Local parks may have their own special attractions; Clissold Park in Hackney has a small zoo while Wimbledon Common has a windmill.

Some parklands are rolling and hilly, and from their summits it is possible to survey the city landscape and pick out familiar profiles like the Post Office Tower and St Paul's Cathedral. Primrose Hill, once a site for early morning duellists, was once part of Regent's Park, and gives a fine view towards the West End. The top of Parliament Hill in Hampstead Heath affords a similarly good view, and is also a popular spot for kite-flying in the summer and tobogganing in the winter snows.

Previous pages: *The view from the top of Primrose Hill looks over Regent's Park towards London's West End.*
Below: *Speakers' Corner, Hyde Park, where any views, however eccentric, may be freely expressed and argued.*
Right: *In quiet contrast are beautiful Kensington Gardens, at the western end of Hyde Park.*

Central London is well-endowed with parkland. Hyde Park, which stretches west from Park Lane and Mayfair, was a wild forested area until Henry VIII enclosed it as a hunting chase. The little River Westbourne that ran through it was damned to become the Serpentine Lake, and vanished underground. The Serpentine has many water birds and other wild creatures living around its shrub-covered islands, and on sunny days it is a popular boating lake. At its eastern end is a large block of granite called The Standing Stone, which was once part of a 19th-Century drinking fountain.

Along the southern edge of Hyde Park stands the barracks of the Household Cavalry, who on occasion may be seen training their horses in the park. Horse riders are a common sight walking or trotting along the track known as Rotten Row – a corruption of 'Route du Roi'. Hyde Park is essentially a people's park and has witnessed many a political gathering and rock concert. It is famous too for Speakers'

Left: The Palm House in the Royal Botanic Gardens at Kew was built to house palm trees from all over the world.

Right: Peace and beauty are not only found in large parks and gardens, but also in small squares like this one in one of West London's residential areas.

Below: Spring blooms in Regent's Park, which is also the home of the London Zoo.

Corner at Marble Arch, where anyone can stand up and say what they please about any subject, to an often more curious than enthralled audience.

West of the Serpentine Bridge is Kensington Gardens, originally part of Hyde Park until William III enclosed his palace garden. This has a more structured and tended feel to it, with avenues of trees, statues, and a peaceful sunken garden enclosing a rectangular pond in front of Kensington Palace. In its childrens' playground stands the familiar statue of Peter Pan; J M Barrie's story was mainly set in these gardens.

Just to the southeast of Hyde Park, St James's Park lies between Buckingham Palace and Horseguards Parade. Several centuries ago it was nothing but a marshy wasteland with a hospital for women lepers. In the 16th Century Henry VIII cleared the area, built St James's Palace, and converted the surrounding space into a deer park. The marsh was later drained and made into a lake, and Charles II turned the land into a formal garden, subsequently landscaped by John Nash in 1828. Today it attracts many visitors, who on sunny days sit in its bright-green deckchairs and sprawl over the grass. In the middle of the weeping willow-fringed lake is Duck Island, the home of numerous birds, including its famous pelicans, who lord it over the lake with a proprietorial air.

Many of London's larger parks were once royal hunting grounds, and Regent's Park is no exception. Originally called Marylebone Park, it was used as such by Charles I, but subsequently Oliver Cromwell sold off its deer and timber to help pay his war debts. Parts were also leased to noblemen, and it was not until the 19th Century that attempts were made to reclaim it as a royal park. It was included in the Prince Regent's plan (hence its name) to build a great neo-classical development designed by John Nash. The main focus was the Inner Circle, which encloses Queen Mary's Garden. This lovely area contains a lake, rockeries and one of the city's most beautiful rose gardens. The park's lakes and

Right: *Across the pond in St James's Park, the spires and roofs of Whitehall rise above the trees.*
Below: *Relaxing on a sunny day in St James's Park.*

boating pond are supplied with water from the Tyburn River, one of several London rivers which run underground. The Grand Union Canal runs through Regent's Park on its way from Little Venice to the Thames at Limehouse. Regent's Park is the home of London Zoo, first opened to the public in 1847, which today contains 6000 living species of animals.

Over on the southwest side of the Thames is Kew Gardens, originally begun two centuries ago by George III's mother, Princess Augusta.

Opposite: The concrete of modern housing contrasts with the vast rural splendour of Richmond Park, once a royal hunting ground. Below: A mounted policeman patrols the hilly terrain of Hampstead Heath. Open-air concerts are held here in summer.

Here, the Royal Botanic Gardens has 300 acres containing exotic plants from all over the world. It is a delight to wander round and admire its flower borders, the Arboretum, the Rock Garden and Decimus Burton's magnificent Palm House, built in 1844–48. Different plants flower throughout the spring and summer; the magnolias in flower are a memorable sight.

West of Kew lies Richmond Park, a vast area which feels far from the city, a feeling emphasized by the herds of deer roaming freely. In the spring it is splashed with the deep mauve of rhododendrons in bloom. It was enclosed as part of Charles I's royal estate, and today it can only be entered through impressive iron gateways on each side. Also south of the Thames but to the east lies Green-

wich Park, where a broad flank of grass rises up to the old Royal Observatory, now a museum. Here too is the meridian, a strip of brass set in stone defining zero degrees longitude from which all longitude measures are taken. The surrounding parkland has some impressive trees, around which run tame grey squirrels, as well as an area called the Wilderness, full of wild flowers and bracken.

Finding a place to breath away from the city bustle does not have to mean a large park. A simple haven is found in the many smaller squares of London, but exemplified in the centre by Soho Square, Tavistock Square and Lincoln's Inn Fields. Here, workers, shoppers and visitors alike can sit amidst grass and flowers and take some respite from the pressures of everyday life.

The Square Mile

Within the 616 square miles that makes up Greater London, the one square mile known as the 'City' is the oldest area and one rich in historic tradition. Today it is well-established as one of the world's leading financial and commercial centres, where all the major British and foreign banks and finance houses are represented. The powerful institutions of the Stock Exchange and Lloyds of London have long and illustrious histories in the City. Other famous places also lie within the City boundaries, such as the Mansion House (home of the Lord Mayor), the Guildhall, St Paul's Cathedral, the Tower of London, the Old Bailey court and the Monument.

The City owes its original existence to the Romans, who built a defensive wall around their settlement in AD 190–210, of which only a few parts still exist today. Many familiar place names originated in the old walled city, like Ludgate, Cripplegate and Bishopsgate, which referred to gates leading into the city.

Although much of the City was destroyed in the Great Fire in 1666, and suffered more recent damage during World War II, many historic buildings still remain. Alongside these has sprung up some of Britain's most modern architecture, made of concrete, glass and steel.

To some these seem brutal compared with the classical beauty of many 18th- and 19th-Century buildings, but they nevertheless have a style of their own which reflects the prosperity and growth of this area.

A lot of traditional City sights have almost disappeared. Some of the old markets have vanished, and the characteristic bowler hat is now rarely seen on the streets. Some customs seem to continue forever, such as the election of the Lord Mayor of London. In 1215 King John signed a charter giving the City population – those within the old city walls – the right to elect their own mayor. Today this tradition continues, surrounded by pomp and ceremony. On the second Saturday in November a newly elected Lord Mayor officially takes office and rides to the Royal Courts of Justice in a ceremonial 18th-Century coach. This is drawn by six shire horses, and accompanied by

Previous pages: The top of the Monument provides a panoramic view of the City of London, the financial heartland.
Right: In the centre of the City, traditional and modern styles of architecture stand side by side.
Below: London's tallest building, the National Westminster Tower, soars 600 feet into the sky.

a bodyguard of Pikemen and Musketeers and a procession of colourful floats. This is the City's most spectacular pageantry, dating back at least 600 years.

The Lord Mayor's successor is chosen from candidates nominated by the livery companies who take a central role in the administration of the City. The first of these companies, or guilds, were formed in the 12th Century as friendly societies, created to further their specific trade or business. The oldest is the Weavers, founded in 1184, but the majority date from the 14th Century. The original 12 Great Companies were the Mercers, Grocers, Clothmakers, Fishmongers, Goldsmiths, Skinners, Merchant Taylors, Haberdashers, Salters, Ironmongers, Vintners and Drapers. Today they number 92, the most recent additions being the Builders Merchants (1978) and the Actuaries and Insurers (1979). As the guilds increased in number and influence, they took to wearing distinctive costumes or liveries, still worn today on special occasions. These companies raised money for the construction of the Guildhall. This dates from 1411,

Within the heart of one of the world's leading financial centres, traditional trades still exist.
The Whitbread Brewery, established in 1742, delivers beer to its city pubs by horse and dray.
Right: These pitchforks form part of a display of stable implements.
Opposite: A dray with its consignment of beer barrels.

Below: One of the Brewery's shire horses, which may also be chosen to pull the ceremonial coach of the Lord Mayor of London.

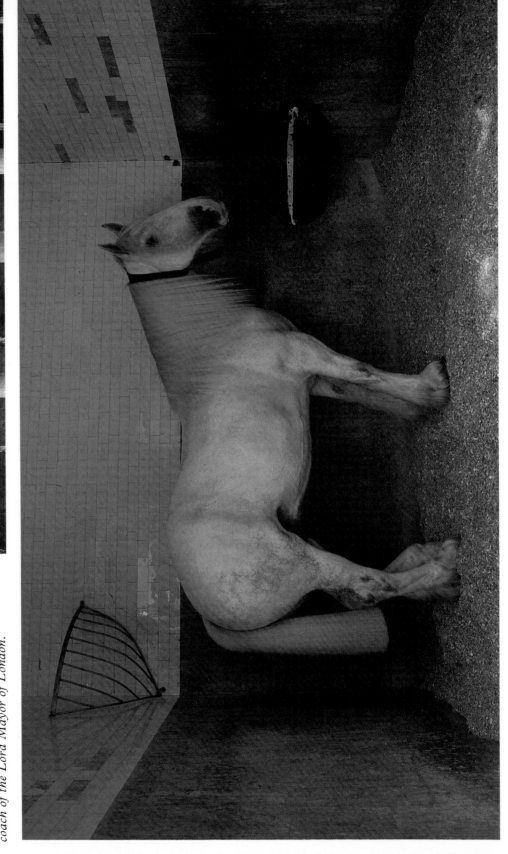

although Wren was responsible for extensive restoration after the Great Fire. Its Great Hall is decorated with the Guilds' shields and banners. As well as administrative functions, the Guilds exert considerable influence over terms of apprenticeships and trade standards.

The City is administered by the Corporation of the City of London via the Court of Common Council, which meets in the Guildhall. It is presided over by the Lord Mayor, and those serving on it are elected by the livery companies from each of the City's 25 wards. This court administers justice within the City; it is the only local authority not elected along party lines, and it is also the only corporation to have

Left: Beer being delivered by horse and dray in the City.
Below left: Every day, over 300,000 commuters pour into London stations like Liverpool Street in the City, where (below) characteristic black taxi cabs wait to whisk them off to the office.

its own police force. Although some of its ancient privileges are now only ceremonial, the City enjoys a great deal of independence, both as a government body and in its business activities.

The City has been the focus of finance and commerce in London since Roman times. In past centuries the city merchants provided the funds for various military campaigns, such as those of Henry V in France. The famous Bank of England building, known as the 'Old lady of Threadneedle Street', was opened in 1734. It was founded in 1694 when city merchants decided to create an independent national bank, but was subsequently nationalized in 1946. Its special responsibilities include printing and issuing bank notes and its vaults are the traditional home of the nation's gold reserves. During the 1780 Gordon Riots the Bank Piquet was set up whereby a detachment of Guards marched every afternoon to the bank and remained on watch throughout the night. This procedure was discontinued in

1973 when an electronic security system was installed.

The City today is undoubtedly one of the most powerful financial centres in the world, and offers the greatest variety of banking, broking, and monetary services to be found anywhere. Nowhere else is it possible to raise such big sums overnight. It is almost impossible to put figures on its daily transactions, but it certainly runs into millions. It is the centre of the world market for bullion, insurance, foreign exchange and shipping, and has one of the biggest stock exchanges in the world.

London was already at the centre of world trade in the 17th Century, with strong overseas links forged by the wool traders and other merchants, and was an important international port. At this time coffee became a popular drink and a number of coffee shops sprang up in the City, particularly around the Royal Exchange, which had opened in 1568 as a meeting place for city merchants. As the shops

were more congenial to meet in than the floor of the Exchange, they gradually became centres for business transactions, and merchants in the same trade tended to meet in the same coffee house. It is not surprising therefore to find that insurance at Lloyds, shipping on the Baltic, and the Stock Exchange (founded in 1773), all had their original premises in coffee houses. This informality meant that much business was conducted on the basis of trust, and still is today, as reflected in the motto of the Stock Exchange, *Dictum Meum Pactum* (My Word is my Bond). On this principle bankers can raise millions of pounds on the strength of a single phone call, and this flexibility, speed and absolute confidence is the key to the City's success.

On the surface the City appears only to come alive during weekdays, when thousands arrive to work in its offices. At night and weekends it seems quiet and empty. In fact there is a growing residential population, and the area has its own university, schools, parks and

gardens. Before World War II, the residential population was only about 2000, but the consequent inner-city reconstruction, mainly the controversial Barbican Project (1959–75), provided homes for 4000–5000 people. The Barbican Centre, a cultural and educational centre, finally opened in 1982. Its theatre is the London home of the Royal Shakespeare Company, and the Guildhall School of Music and Drama. The City also contains other theatres, as well as restaurants, pubs, clubs, newspapers, churches, hospitals and markets. It may seem to be dominated by the buildings and business of high-level finance, but a closer look reveals a thriving local community and a wealth of history.

Previous pages: The floor of the London Stock Exchange, where millions of shares are traded every day.
Opposite: Dirty Dick's provides a welcome venue for local office workers, while the Wig and Pen Club (right) in the Strand, is mainly frequented by barristers and journalists.
Below: The towering blocks of the Barbican development, seen here with St Giles, Cripplegate, in the foreground.

A Place of Worship

In the noisy bustle of city traffic, the sounds of church bells are muffled and lost. Yet on Sundays their peels ring out clearly, summoning people to worship as they have done for hundreds of years. London has numerous churches of various sizes and denominations, many with extremely long histories. Apart from their architectural interest, they offer finely crafted statues, stained glass windows and woodcarving.

The spires of London's churches used to dominate the skyline in the days when the city and its buildings were much smaller. Many of these churches were destroyed in the Great Fire of 1666, and those that were rebuilt from the ashes were predominantly designed by Sir Christopher Wren. Some 51 parish churches were designed by Wren in name, although in fact he had several collaborators. These churches were all very different from one another, and from his greatest masterpiece, St Paul's Cathedral. He made a distinction between the noble theme of the cathedral and the more everyday ones of ordinary churches. St Paul's had to dominate the city and become a monument *par excellence*. Today, even though

Previous pages: St Paul's Cathedral, Wren's best-known masterpiece, completed in 1710, took 35 years to build. The richly decorated ceiling above the High Altar (left) and this unusual view of the dome (below) are only two aspects of its great beauty and craftsmanship.

it has lost its status as the tallest building, it still presents a striking profile among London's tall office blocks.

However St Paul's history precedes Wren. It dates back to AD 604 when the Pope sent missionaries to England, including Mellitus, who was installed in the first little wooden cathedral-church of St Paul's. It was destroyed by fire several times before the Normans began building a replacement in the 11th Century. When completed in the 13th Century it became the focus of religious life in London. Its importance declined over the following centuries, and by the early 1600s it was said to be 'frequented by cutpurses, whores, card-sharps, quack doctors, marriage brokers and drunks.' Its aisles were lined with tradesmen's stalls, and it was used as a short cut by horse-drawn carts. Inigo Jones was commissioned to restore it, but the Civil War put a stop to that, and during the war the Parliamentarians used it to stable their horses. After the Restoration Charles II asked Wren to draw up plans to completely remodel it, but before this could happen it was destroyed by the Great Fire.

Wren's first designs were rejected as too new-fangled – he originally proposed a Greek cross – and his subsequent approved designs took many years to complete. The first stone was laid in 1675 and the final one in 1710 with Wren supervising every operation. The placing of the magnificent dome was a remarkable feat of engineering. One of its unplanned features

is the famous 'Whispering Gallery', where a message whispered into the wall on one side can be heard clearly 112 feet away on the other side. Some of the choir stalls are carved by the renowned wood carver Grinling Gibbons. The cathedral originally contained no monuments, but gradually these accumulated. The North Aisle is dominated by a memorial to the Duke of Wellington. He is buried in the Crypt, together with other famous people including Lord Nelson. Wren himself was buried there in 1723 and his tomb bears the epitaph, in Latin, 'Reader, if you seek his monument, look about you.'

Wren also designed many other well-known London churches, some of which have tall distinctive spires. St Brides in Fleet Street is known as the 'Church of the Press' or the 'Journalists' Church'. It was extensively damaged in 1940 during the Blitz and all that remained was its façade and beautifully tiered steeple. During its restoration interesting remains of much-earlier buildings were discovered, including a 6th-Century Saxon church, now on view in the crypt. Another

Opposite: Looking down the wide nave of the Brompton Oratory, a Roman Catholic Church in Knightsbridge.
Below: St Brides in Fleet Street, also designed by Wren, is known as 'The Journalists' Church'.

distinctive Wren church is St Clement Danes in the Strand, whose origins date to the 9th Century. Rebuilt by Wren in the 1680s, it was rebuilt again after World War II. It is the memorial church of the Royal Air Force and the flooring contains the crests of some 900 squadrons and Commonwealth air forces. It too has a fine, tall steeple, containing the bells referred to in the nursery rhyme – 'Oranges and lemons say the bells of St Clements'. Another Wren church immortalized for its bells is St Mary-le-Bow, Cheapside. Bow Bells once rang as a curfew, and it is said that only those born within their sound are true Cockneys.

St Martin-in-the-Fields is an outstanding 18th-Century church in Trafalgar Square. Originally a medieval church surrounded by open fields, it was redesigned by James Gibbs. He positioned the lovely steeple over the centre of the portico. He provided ample gallery space for the congregation and a royal box for George I, since Buckingham Palace comes within its parish boundaries. Its vaulted crypt is opened every night as a refuge for homeless people. This tradition was started by H R L Sheppard, an army chaplain who, after his return from World War I, always kept the church open for stranded servicemen and other homeless people.

Westminster Cathedral is Britain's main Roman Catholic cathedral, built between 1895

and 1903, in an Italian-Byzantine style. Its interior is decorated with red, yellow and white marble, and it has the widest nave in England. Another beautiful Roman Catholic church is Brompton Oratory, designed by Herbert Gribble and built between 1880 and 1884. Constructed with Portland stone, it resembles a 16th-Century North Italian church. It is light and spacious and its broad nave is 51 feet wide. Its lavish mosaic decorations were added in the 1930s. It contains several treasures rescued from other churches, including lifesize statues of the 12 Apostles by Giuseppe Mazzuoli.

Westminster Abbey has been the coronation place of all 39 English Sovereigns since William the Conqueror in 1066 (except Edward V and Edward VIII who were never crowned). It was originally the site of a Benedictine Abbey, called the West Monastery; hence its name. Rebuilt by Edward the Confessor in the 11th Century, it was not finished until 1269 and was modelled on French cathedrals such as Reims. It is shaped like a Latin cross and is over 500 feet long and over 200 feet wide. The twin towers, which are 225 feet high, were added by Nicholas Hawksmoor in the 18th Century. Its Henry VII Chapel has a beautiful, intricate fan-vaulted ceiling, as well as flying buttresses and delicately shaped walls. The Abbey contains about 1000 monuments, which tend to hinder any clear appreciation of its

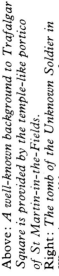

Above: A well-known background to Trafalgar Square is provided by the temple-like portico of St Martin-in-the-Fields.
Right: The tomb of the Unknown Soldier in Westminster Abbey commemorates those unknown soldiers who died in World War I.

architectural merits. These commemorate many great names from British history, such as ex-prime ministers like Peel, Palmerston, Disraeli and Gladstone, while Poets' Corner remembers such people as Shakespeare, Milton, Wordsworth, Keats and Shelley.

There are countless churches to explore that have interesting associations. For instance, it was from the top of All-Hallows-by-the-Tower that Samuel Pepys watched the Great Fire, and he is buried in St Olaves, a church he helped to save from the Fire by having the surrounding buildings demolished. St Sepulchre in Holborn is known as the 'Musicians Church', and St Mary, Rotherhithe, has strong associations with the sea and sailors. Whatever your religious views, it is not possible to enter many of London's churches without admiring the level of artistry and craftsmanship which they have reached, and the rich history that they have been witness to.

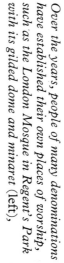

Over the years, people of many denominations have established their own places of worship, such as the London Mosque in Regent's Park with its gilded dome and minaret (left),

All Saints Greek Orthodox Church in Camden Town (above), and St Peter's in Clerkenwell which was built to serve the local Italian population (below).

College of the Ouach

L ondon attracts shoppers like moths to a flame, whether for cashmere sweaters, tailor-made suits, cotton underwear or sophisticated hi-fi equipment. Most visitors to the city do not leave without a shopping spree, and some visit expressly for that purpose. London has achieved a reputation as the shopping centre of Europe, and not without reason since it offers such a wide variety of goods, and the opportunity to explore a diverse range of shops and markets.

For more exclusive shoppers, surely one of the most familiar names is that of Harrods, Knightsbridge. The largest departmental store in Europe, it claims to be able to provide anything that anyone could possibly wish to buy, from gold paperclips to a fresh octopus, a Bechstein piano to a jar of truffles. It has a style and tradition all its own, and is an attractive place just to wander around, especially the superbly decorated Food Hall. Knightsbridge is the home of many exclusive shops, as is Mayfair, where it is still possible to find hatters and tailors in Savile Row, the established centre for tailor-made gentlemen's clothes for over a century. Before mass-produced suits took over the market, any well-to-do-gentleman would visit his tailor and arrange to be fitted with the best suit his money could buy.

Mayfair and Piccadilly also offer several old-fashioned arcades such as Burlington Arcade,

Previous pages: Camden Lock market, a colourful weekend market of shops and stalls specializing in arts and crafts.

Opposite: At night, Harrods' illuminated exterior is one of Knightsbridge's most well-known landmarks.

Below: The beautifully tiled Food Hall at Harrods is famous for its wide range of fish, meat, poultry and game.

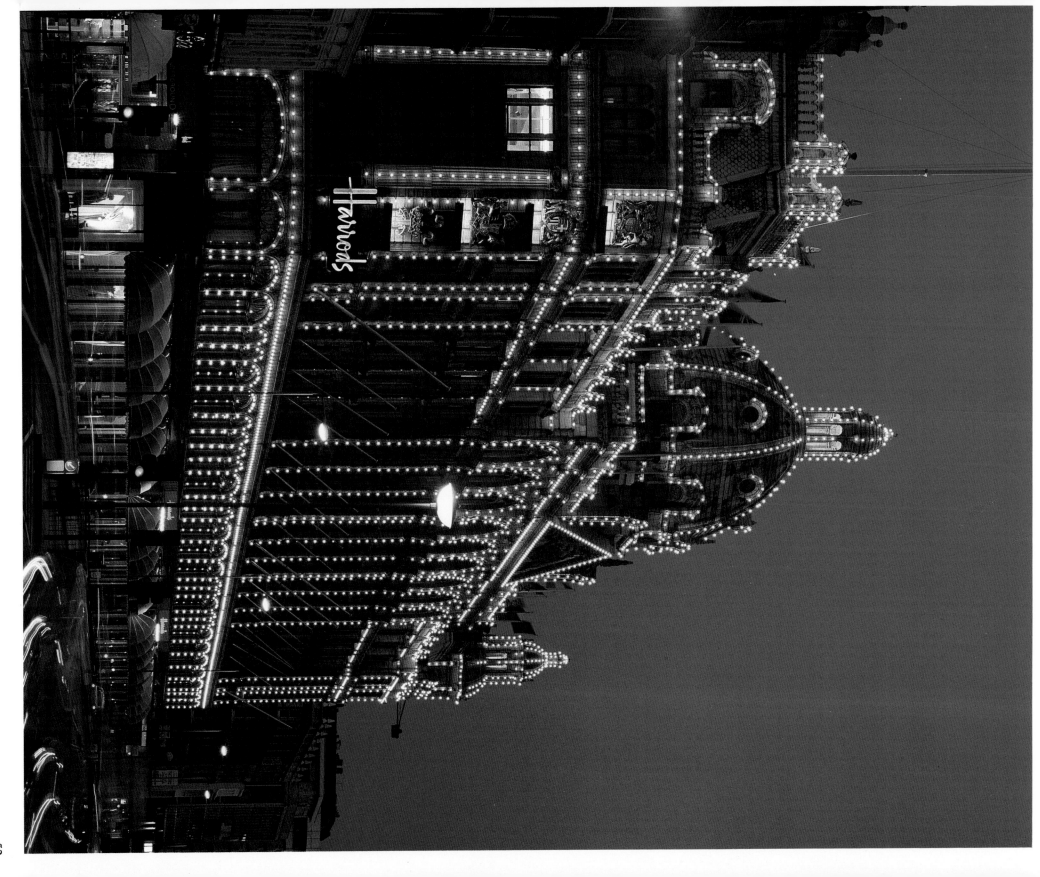

Above: Selfridges is Oxford Street's best-known department store.
Left: Royal Arcade, Mayfair, is one of several shopping malls specializing in exclusive goods.
Below: Covent Garden, once a busy fruit and vegetable market, is now a fashionable shopping and entertainment centre.

Nearby Bond Street is also a fashionable shopping area. Divided into Old and New Bond Street, built in 1686 and 1700 respectively, its shops specialize in fine art, antiques and jewellery. It is the home of Cartier, the jewellers, and Sotheby's, the famous auctioneers. Founded by Samuel Baker in 1744, Sotheby's first sale was a library for £826. Nowadays, its sales run into millions of pounds. Savory and Moore, recognizable by its elegant Georgian façade, is said to be the oldest chemist's shop in London.

Piccadilly Arcade and Royal Arcade. Burlington Arcade, one of the oldest, contains many small shops specializing in antiques, tobacco, handmade shirts, jewellery and cashmere.

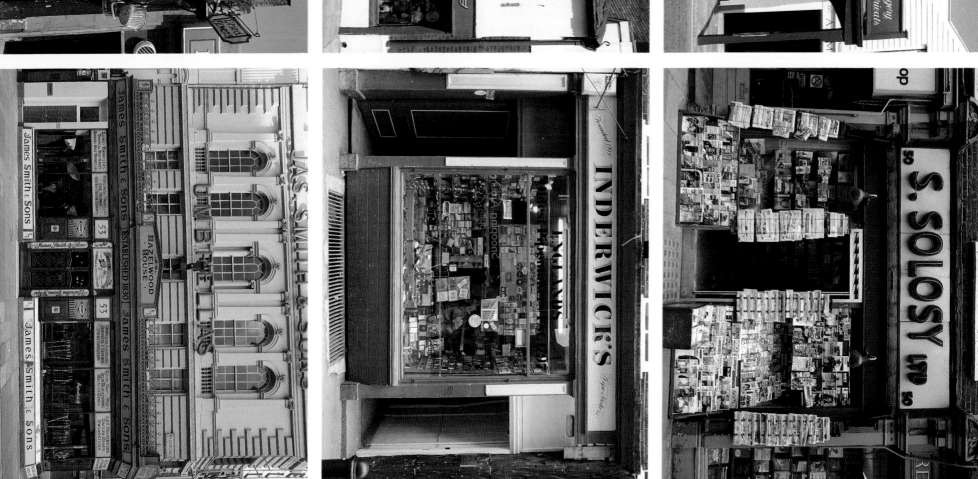

Previous pages: *A selection of London's many and varied shops.*
Opposite: *Of London's major wholesale markets, only Spitalfields and Smithfield (below) still operate on their original sites.*

Other old shops that have preserved their distinctive decor and atmosphere can be found tucked away in the city centre. In Jermyn Street, Piccadilly, is the small 18th-Century shop of Floris the perfumiers, while further up the road, Paxton and Whitfield is an old cheese shop whose aroma attracts many a gourmet. In nearby St James's Street, James Lock the hatters have been established for over 200 years and are responsible for making the first bowler hat. Inderwicks in Carnaby Street are England's oldest pipe-makers, dating from 1797 and they sell all types from briars to hookahs. Over in Lincoln's Inn Fields, the Old Curiosity Shop is an antique shop dating from around the 17th Century which claims to have been the model for Charles Dickens' novel of the same name.

In more recent times, the shopping streets that have attained fame are Carnaby Street, and Kings Road, Chelsea. Carnaby Street

became fashionable in the 1960s, when the upsurge of youth culture and rock music resulted in an expanding market for new fashion images. At this time Mary Quant created a new look in hair, clothes and make-up and opened the first boutique in the Kings Road. Today Carnaby Street seems rather outdated, but Kings Road is still a lively shopping area where some of the most eccentric styles are originated and worn.

Covent Garden is an area of central London that has been totally transformed over the past twelve years. Once the city's principal fruit, vegetable and flower market, it is now a chic shopping centre, full of boutiques, arts and crafts shops, wine bars, restaurants and street entertainers. Its name dates back to before the 16th Century, when the monks of Westminster Abbey had a walled garden there. It changed hands after the dissolution of the monasteries and in 1631 the Earl of Bedford commissioned Inigo Jones to design houses for the gentry to be set around an Italian-style piazza. Its square and covered walks attracted traders from miles around and by the end of the century it had become the site of a lively and successful market, and so noisy that many

residents vacated their homes to shopkeepers. Recognized as an important fruit and vegetable market, a custom-built market-place was erected in 1830, which was soon spilling over with traders. In the mid-20th Century the decision was taken to move it to Nine Elms; the move took place in 1974. Today Covent Garden retains its Tuscan portico and the original Regency shopfronts which are now thronged by shoppers seeking a different sort of merchandise.

London still has many colourful and busy street markets where you can buy everything from meat, fish, fruit and vegetables to clothes, china, saucepans and expensive antiques. The Portobello Road in West London has been known for its antiques since the 1950s, although it has been a general market street for centuries. In the 1960s and 70s it became a popular hippy area and there was a lively exchange of old clothes, jewellery and Victoriana. Today its Saturday market has stalls and shops selling all kinds of furniture, books, records, jewellery, toys, medals and general junk which attracts a wide variety of customers.

Petticoat Lane Market in East London was once the home of carpenters and glaziers, but

59

Above: Saturday is the busiest time in the Portobello Road antique market, while Petticoat Lane market (right) only operates on a Sunday.

is now full of cut-price warehouses. It got its name in the 17th Century from the large numbers of old-clothes dealers who assembled there and, despite changing its name to Middlesex Street in 1846, the market has never lost its familiar name. Famous for the patter used by stall-holders selling their wares, today its traditional Cockney atmosphere is intermingled with that of the Jewish, Asian and West Indian communities who also inhabit the area. At the Sunday market, it is possible to buy almost any kind of household goods and clothing.

Billingsgate, Smithfield and Spitalfields have long been associated with important trade markets. Smithfield is the city's main wholesale meat market, where over 200,000 tons of meat is sold every year. Its name is a corruption of 'Smoothfield' – it was an open space just outside the old city walls. It was the scene of tournaments, fairs and horse and cattle markets from the 12th to the 19th Century. St Bartholemew's Fair, one of England's most important cloth fairs of the Middle Ages, was held here every August and attracted people from all over Europe. It has a less happy association as a place of execution, where nearly 300 people were burned at the

stake during Queen Mary's reign. The present Smithfield building was designed by Sir Horace Jones in the mid-19th Century, in a Renaissance style of red-brick with iron and glass arcades, flanked by domed towers.

Spitalfields Market in East London sells fruit and vegetables from all over the world. It dates from the 17th Century but the present market building was not opened until 1928. Now modernized, the traditional wooden hand barrows are still used. The oldest market in London, Billingsgate fish market was sited on the north bank of the Thames until 1982, when it moved to the Isle of Dogs. The porters are known for their strange leather hats, which enable them to carry boxes on their heads, and for their coarse language, which has made Billingsgate a synonym for abuse.

A cosmopolitan city, London contains many established ethnic communities who have their own shops selling their own specific food and other merchandise. Soho's Gerrard Street is London's Chinatown, full of Chinese restaurants and supermarkets, and East London's Brick Lane is associated with Indian shops and restaurants. Many other kinds of shops are to be found, specializing for instance in Jewish, Greek, Italian, Japanese and even Latin American goods. These are scattered in a variety of locations in London and illustrate that it can also be fruitful and often a lot more interesting to explore shops and markets away from the crowded city centre.

All the Queen's Men

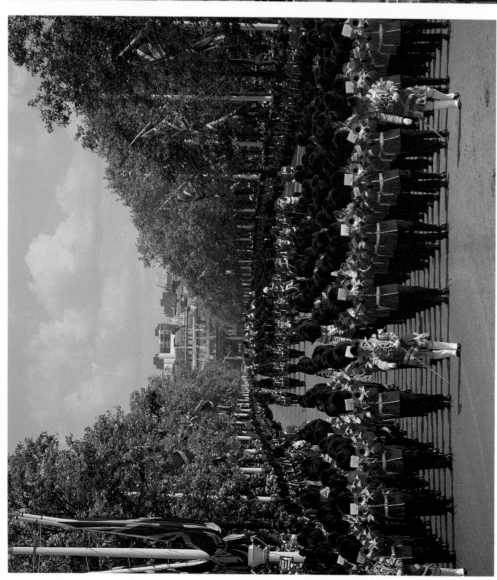

Previous pages: Guards assemble at Wellington Barracks in Birdcage Walk to take part in the Trooping of the Colour. Above: Led by the State Trumpeter, the bands of the Guards Regiments return from Horse Guards Parade to Buckingham Palace, where they are saluted by Her Majesty The Queen (right).

London's pageantry is a national institution, providing elaborate and colourful ceremonies that never disappoint the assembled crowds. Even the chance glimpse of a small procession of Life Guards riding from their Hyde Park barracks down Constitution Hill and along The Mall is a compelling sight. The sun glints off their helmets, plumes flow in the wind, and scarlet tunics contrast vividly with the coats of sleek black horses as they go to mount guard at Horse Guards. They present a sense of history and a richness of colour, pomp and ceremony that has little in common with today's military image of camouflage uniforms and armoured tanks.

The ancient ceremony of Changing of the Guard is performed almost every day by the troops of the Household Division, an 8000-strong force who are the Sovereign's personal bodyguard. Two mounted regiments provide the guard in Horse Guards, Whitehall, and five regiments of Foot Guards stand guard at Buckingham Palace, St James's Palace and at the Tower of London, where they guard the entrance and the Jewel House. Every evening they carry out the Ceremony of the Keys; the Chief Yeoman Warder, carrying the Queen's Keys, symbolically locks up the Tower.

The Queen's Guards are not solely engaged in these ceremonial activities, as some people assume. They are fighting soldiers with a long and active history and, at any one time, half are on overseas service. Their colours display their past battle honours, which range from the defence of Tangier in 1680 to El Alamein and other battles of World War II.

The Foot Guards are made up of regiments of Grenadier, Coldstream, Scots, Irish and Welsh Guards. The older regiments once had their own uniforms and colours but in the mid-19th Century they adopted the familiar dress of scarlet tunic, dark-blue trousers with a red stripe and black bearskin head-dress. At first glance they seem identical, but closer inspection reveals differences in the colours of the plumes in their bearskins, and the motifs on their badges. The Irish Guards, for example, have a blue plume and a shamrock on their badge, while the Welsh Guards have a white plume and their badge shows the leek – the national emblem of Wales. The Coldstream Guards have a red plume, and the Grenadier Guards have a collar badge in the form of a grenade.

The Queen's Life Guards are the mounted regiments of the Household Division, made up of the Life Guards and the Blues and Royals (the Royal Horse Guards and 1st Dragoons). One regiment is stationed at Windsor while the other is overseas, but each also provides a mounted squadron of 128 horses to perform traditional ceremonial duties. Each guard only has a short term of duty with the mounted

Previous pages: The drum horse and the massed mounted bands of the Household Cavalry take their positions before marching to Horse Guards Parade for the Trooping of the Colour.

Left: The Yeomen of the Guard in full ceremonial dress are inspected before attending their annual Whitsunday church service. The two uniforms of the Yeomen of the Guard contrast (right) the more-sombre colours of everyday dress and (below) the brilliant scarlet-and-gold livery worn on ceremonial occasions.

regiment and then returns to duties with his respective armoured regiment.

The mounted guard dates back to the 17th Century, when a band of loyal men formed a bodyguard for the exiled King Charles II. Like the Foot Guards, there are differences between the regimental uniforms; the Blues and Royals wear dark-blue tunics and a red-plumed helmet, as contrasted with the bright-red tunics and white plumes worn by the Life Guards. Both wear polished steel cuirasses (breastplates) – the last British troops to wear

armour. Their horses are traditionally black, except for those of the State Trumpeters, which are grey, and the drumhorses who lead the Regimental Bands, which are heavier in build and have skewbald or piebald markings.

The Guards are involved in several annual

to the throne in the House of Lords to deliver her speech outlining government proposals for the new session.

Whether standing on guard or on parade, Guards have to exercise extreme control. They have to stand for long periods scarcely moving a muscle, they cannot scratch their nose, cough or sneeze, smile or laugh, or indulge any of the small reflexes we do without thinking. Sometimes on a very hot day, this can prove too much for even the best-drilled soldier, and guards have been known to faint. As befits his training, however, a good soldier will not collapse in a heap but will fall standing to attention and be carried discreetly away.

Such pageantry and the Royal Family itself seem like anachronisms in today's society. Kings, queens, princes and princesses are the stuff of fairytales, yet they exert endless fascination for ordinary people. A Royal wedding dominates news and conversation for months, and costs a fortune, but this is more than repaid in tourist revenue and as a spectacular and opportune diversion in times of economic recession. All the Queen's horses and all the Queen's men may not have put Humpty Dumpty together again but they contribute to the British economy and are a colourful part of London's heritage.

pageants. Probably the most magnificent military display in the country is the Trooping of the Colour, held on the Queen's official birthday in June. This ceremony has been performed since 1755 but only became linked with the Sovereign's birthday later, in 1805. Each regiment of Foot Guards takes it in turn for its colour to be 'trooped', a practice originally designed to teach the men to recognize their own regimental colours. The Queen, in the uniform of one of the regiments of which she is Colonel-in-Chief, rides from Buckingham Palace to Horse Guards Parade, where the massed regiments of the Brigade of Guards and the Household Cavalry are waiting. After she has taken the salute, there is a marching display and the trooping of the selected colour.

Another ceremonial occasion is the State Opening of Parliament, when the Queen rides to Westminster in the Irish State Coach. Here she dons the royal robes and crown and ascends

The Life Guards, seen here on duty in Whitehall (left) and outside Buckingham Palace (below), are distinguishable by the white plumes of their helmets and their bright-red jackets.

Opposite: A soldier of the Scots Guards stands on duty outside St James's Palace.

A Wealth of Culture

Over the many centuries of its existence London has gained a rich cultural heritage, explorable through its historic buildings which have many tales to unfold, its art galleries and museums, concert halls and theatres.

In Trafalgar Square the National Gallery has some of the world's finest masterpieces, representing schools of painting from many countries. Many peaceful hours may be spent wandering slowly past beautiful works by such great masters as Botticelli, Rembrandt, Rubens, Goya, Manet and Renoir. Nearby is the National Portrait Gallery, housing one of the most comprehensive collections of portraits of famous men and women, as well as sculptures, miniatures, engravings and photographs.

The full excellence of the English School of painting has to be appreciated at the Tate Gallery on Millbank. Here a permanent collection of British art displays works from the Elizabethan era up to the early 20th Century, including almost 300 canvases from the Turner bequest. Sir Francis Chantrey, a 19th-Century sculptor, had the idea of creating a collection of British art and bequeathed his fortune for just that purpose. The amount of art subsequently gathered together obviously needed a special gallery. Sir Henry Tate, the sugar magnate, stepped in to finance the project, resulting in the present gallery, which opened in 1897. It is also well-endowed with foreign artists including Cezanne, Matisse, Picasso, Braque and Klee, and its exhibitions of modern art have occasionally caused much controversy.

Many smaller galleries are scattered over the city, and hunting down some of the less central ones can be very rewarding, as in the case of Leighton House Art Gallery in Holland Park. Built in 1866 by the artist Lord Leighton, its exotic interior includes a lavishly ornate Arab Room decorated with tiles from Rhodes, Damascus and Cairo. Over in Walthamstow, East London, the William Morris Gallery is devoted to the fascinating life and work of this 19th-Century artist, poet and free-thinker.

The Hayward Gallery, which plays host to temporary art exhibitions, opened in 1968 as part of the South Bank complex. In the 1930s this relatively neglected area was seen as ripe for development in a new and challenging way, but World War II delayed progress and it was not until the 1940s that plans were drawn up for an arts centre. The site was chosen for the Festival of Britain and consequently the Festival Hall, a stark, grey, concrete building, opened in 1951. Its modern architecture still

Previous pages: The Albert Hall, Knightsbridge, is the venue for a variety of meetings and musical performances, the best-known of which are the Henry Wood Promenade Concerts.

Opposite: This elegant glass-domed room inside The British Museum is the main reading room of The British Library.

Below: The Tate Gallery, on Millbank, houses some of Britain's major art collections.

Above: The controversial geometric architecture of the National Theatre on the South Bank presents a stark contrast to the curved beauty of the dome of St Paul's in the background.

Right: Surprisingly tucked away in residential West London, Leighton House contains a colourfully tiled Arab Hall, shown here.

stands out prominently, and its balconies afford fine views over the river Thames. At night, reflected lights flicker in the water, and familiar city profiles like the Houses of Parliament and St Paul's show up clearly on the skyline. The success of the Festival of Britain increased interest in expanding the arts centre, resulting in the Queen Elizabeth Hall, the National Film Theatre, and the Hayward Gallery. The National Theatre was a later addition, following the formation of the National Theatre Company under the joint directorship of Sir Laurence Olivier and Sir John Guilgud. A bare concrete building, both inside and out, it presents a great contrast to the lush interiors of most West End theatres.

London's Albert Hall, named after Queen Victoria's consort, Prince Albert, was partly financed by money left over from building the Albert Memorial, and was opened in 1871. It is a vast circular, red-brick building, covered with a glass and iron dome decorated with

terracotta and a mosaic frieze illustrating triumphs of art and science. Although it is particularly well-known for the Promenade Concerts (the 'Proms') founded by Sir Henry Wood in 1895, it is the venue for a diverse range of other entertainments including rock concerts and boxing and tennis tournaments.

Prince Albert was responsible for creating the magnificent museums situated in and around Exhibition Road. His enthusiastic support helped promote the highly successful Great Exhibition, held in Hyde Park in 1851, and on his suggestion the resulting profits

were used to buy land on which to build educational establishments. By 1856 work on this project had already begun. The Museum of Manufactures, originally part of the Exhibition, expanded to form the basis of the Victoria and Albert Museum, which opened in 1909. Today this is the national museum for fine and applied art, covering a range of periods and styles, and containing a delightful mixture of both serious and more frivolous exhibits.

Exploring science becomes instantly enjoyable as well as accessible in the Science Museum. A favourite section with adults and children alike is the one where things move, light up, or make noises at the press of a button or turn of a knob. Just around the corner, the buff-and-blue terracotta façade of the Natural History Museum is covered with carvings of animals and plants, while inside, its vast collection includes every species of animal from the tiniest mouse to huge dinosaurs and whales, as well as birds, fish, insects and plants.

Some of the world's richest treasures are found in the British Museum – the Elgin Marbles are there, the Rosetta stone from Egypt, several Egyptian mummies and two of

Left: The imposing entrance to the Natural History Museum in South Kensington. The museum contains an unrivalled collection of different species. One of the most popular is a skeleton and life-size model of the Blue Whale (below).

the original copies of the Magna Carta. The present museum was specially built on the site of the old one which by the early 1800s had become far too small. It was constructed around a central courtyard, which was almost immediately roofed over to form the famous domed Reading Room. Since 1973 this has come under the auspices of The British Library, and contains an amazing 110 miles of shelving, and libraries of music and maps.

The scales of 'Justice' surmount the Old Bailey, London's Central Criminal Court, built on the site of the notorious Newgate Prison. This has been the scene of many famous and dramatic trials, involving murder and high treason. Less serious cases however are brought to the Royal Courts of Justice, at the junction of Fleet Street and the Strand. This extensive building is adorned with details drawn from architecture of the Middle Ages, and has deep pointed archways and round turrets that protrude out of the walls above the pavement. The surrounding areas contain the Inns of Court, originally founded for the education and lodgings of lawyers. These peaceful havens retain an old-fashioned atmosphere in complete contrast to the bustling streets outside. There used to be twelve Inns of Court but only three still exist in their traditional capacity; Gray's Inn, Lincoln's Inn and Temple. Black-gowned, white-wigged barristers striding across the courtyards are a common sight.

On an island in the Strand, outside the church of St Clement Danes, stands the statue of Dr Samuel Johnson. An eminent scholar, his quotations about the city of London in the 18th Century have earned him a place in history. He is famous too for his dictionary, which took him 8½ years to write and contained 40,000 words. In 1763 he struck up a firm friendship with James Boswell, a diarist, whose chronicle recorded many of the quotations attributed to Johnson.

The most well-known diarist must be Samuel Pepys, who began keeping his daily notes, in cipher, around 1660, while he was working for the Admiralty. Unfortunately, by 1669 his failing eyesight had curtailed these writings, but not before he had produced more than a million words describing the graphic details of life in 17th-Century London under Charles II. Not only did he record

ordinary life and people, but he also bore witness to the Coronation, the Plague and the Great Fire of London.

The country's main political activity is centred around Westminster, in the Houses of Parliament, and in the government offices in Whitehall and Downing Street, where many crucial decisions are made. Important issues of the day are debated and voted upon in the House of Commons and the House of Lords. In the Commons, the governing and opposition parties face one another, while the Speaker sits at one end acting as chairman. When a vote is taken, Members of Parliament file into lobbies, the 'Ayes' to the right and the 'Noes' to the left. Today the Commons has almost total authority for national government although some Bills go on to be amended in the Lords

and returned to the Commons. England has been governed from Westminster for over nine centuries. The Commons evolved in the 14th Century under Edward III, when officers of State were elected by the monarch. A system of parliamentary majority was set up at the end of the 17th Century and Robert Walpole subsequently became the country's first Prime Minister, thus establishing the system we are familiar with today.

Below: *The Georgian splendour of Lincoln's Inn, which accommodates the offices of many lawyers and solicitors.*

Opposite: *This clothmaker's house opposite St Bartholomew's Church, near Smithfield, is one of the few buildings to survive the Great Fire of London.*

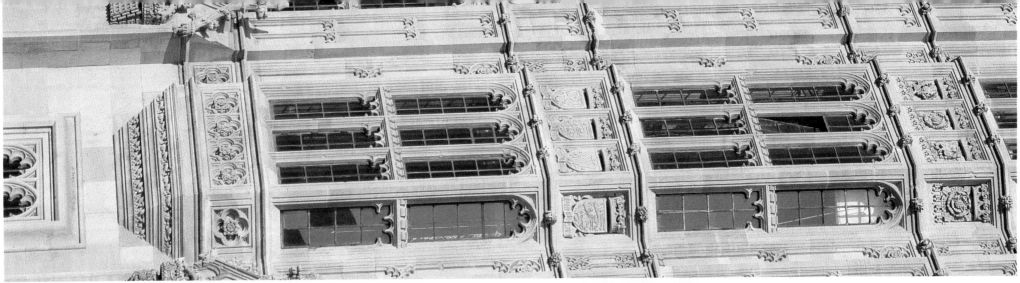

Left: In Old Palace yard outside the Houses of Parliament stands a bronze statue of Richard I.
Below: The vaulted arches of Lincoln's Inn behind the Law Courts.

Above: 'He who is tired of London is tired of life, for there is in London all that life can afford.' These were the famous words of Dr Samuel Johnson, whose statue stands outside the Law Courts in the Strand.

Leisurely Pursuits

T he gentle 'thwack' of leather on willow and a soft ripple of applause are instantly recognizable sounds, reminders of sunny summer days when cricket is played on the local green. It is a delightfully English game, seemingly slow and sedate, yet the skilful force of the bowler and the batsman provide moments of excitement every bit as great as in more active games. The players' 'whites' show up distinctly against the well-tended green grass, and clusters of spectators sit around the edge, lazily chatting or enjoying picnics. Although cricket is traditionally associated with the village green, it is widely played in

London. The two best-known places for national and international matches are the Oval in Kennington, home of the Surrey County Cricket Club, and Lords Cricket Ground in St John's Wood, home of both the Middlesex County Cricket Club and Marylebone Cricket Club, better known as the MCC. Both these grounds are venues for Test Matches, when England plays the other Test countries – Australia, New Zealand, the West Indies, India and Pakistan. Britain introduced cricket to these countries in the days when it was an important colonial power. Cricket originated in England among shepherds using

their crooks as bats, and formal rules were not drawn up until the mid-18th Century.

London is well endowed with sporting activities: its football clubs play every week, climaxing in the FA Cup Final held at

Previous pages: Lords Cricket Ground is the home of Middlesex Cricket Club, seen here playing a match against the Australian cricket team.

Opposite: Street entertainment has become a regular feature of Covent Garden, which has also seen the blossoming of restaurants and bars (below).

Wembley; rugby enthusiasts are geared towards the championship final held at Twickenham; and for tennis fans, Wimbledon means only one thing – two weeks of excitement when tennis players from all over the world assemble to compete for the most coveted prizes and championship status. During these two weeks, strawberries and cream and necks stiff from turning are the order of the day.

An event that also only takes place once a year is the Boat Race, one of London's best-known sporting occasions. On a Saturday just before Easter, two crews of eight rowers and a coxswain representing the Universities of Oxford and Cambridge race the four miles of the River Thames from Putney to Mortlake. The first Boat Race took place in 1829 at Henley-on-Thames, and was won by Oxford. At present, Cambridge is in the lead, having won 68 times to Oxford's 62, and both have suffered the indignity of sinking before finishing the course. Traditionally crewed by men, both teams have introduced women coxes in recent years, Oxford in 1981 and Cambridge in 1985. It is a most enjoyable scene to watch on a fine Spring day, as each crew struggles to draw a few feet ahead, oars dipping rhythmically in the water, urged on by the slight figure of the cox sitting in the stern, and pursued by a flotilla of small craft crowded with enthusiastic spectators.

Some people prefer to mess around in boats in a more relaxed way, taking a boat down the Thames at Richmond for instance, or having a trip on a colourfully painted narrow boat along the canal in Regent's Park. Part of the Grand Union Canal, this waterway was opened in 1820. The London section runs from the junction with the Paddington Canal in Little Venice, all the way through Regent's Park and Camden Town to Limehouse, where it meets the Thames. At Camden Lock, it runs next to the busy weekend arts, crafts, antiques and clothes market, and on sunny days the stretch of water between here and Little Venice is chock-a-block with slow-moving craft.

A rather speedier set of boats is moored at the marina on St Katharine Dock, in the shadow of Tower Bridge. Since this dock was closed in 1968, the area has been developed and the warehouses restored for a variety of purposes. It has been transformed into a place where people come to stroll around the marinas and the floating museum of unusual watercraft, eat and drink at the Dickens Inn overlooking the river, and perhaps pay a visit to the Tower of London.

Below: Morris dancers perform outside the Dickens Inn at St Katharine Dock, part of which has been redeveloped as a marina (opposite).

Previous pages: *Some of the people who make up London's varied population.*

Opposite: *The tranquillity of life on Regent's Park canal.*

Right: *Soho Square, like many of London's West End squares, provides an outdoor place to have lunch for many local workers.*

Below: *At Camden Lock, passengers disembark after their trip down the canal on a narrow boat.*

Alongside St Katharine Dock on the river is Wapping, where the vast London docks, built in the early 1800s, are now being re-developed for residential use. It is also the site of one of the oldest riverside pubs, the Prospect of Whitby, part of which dates from 1520. Once an infamous haunt of river pirates called The Devil's Tavern, it was also frequently visited by Samuel Pepys when he was Secretary to The Admiralty, and is today the meeting place of the Pepys Society.

There are over 7000 pubs in London, of all types and sizes. These cater for every taste, ranging from small and unassuming, or old and historic, to large and cavernous or modern

93

and noisy. The pub is a British institution and Londoners are no exception in their enjoyment of a good drink with business or for pleasure. Pubs were traditionally divided into the Public Bar – usually bare and smoky, lino on the floor, dartboard on the wall, and a variety of men propping up the bar – and the Lounge or Saloon Bar, with tables and carpeted floors, occupied by both men and women. The Public Bar has become a relatively rare phenomenon, and as pub owners have renovated their premises they have inevitably created two Saloon Bars or merged the two into one. Changes in the role of women have contributed to this, and while it was previously unusual to find women drinking in pubs, especially unaccompanied by men, nowadays, in London at least, it is a normal occurrence.

Many London pubs now offer entertainment. Once this consisted of striptease, drag artists, variety competitions and a three-piece band playing old favourites, but more recently pubs have become centres for up-and-coming bands who play to a growing range of listeners.

Right: *Military bands are an ever-popular feature of London's parks.*
Below: *A drink in the sun at the Anglesea Arms, Chelsea.*

94

Another development has been fringe theatre, pioneered by the King's Head in Islington, and the Duke of Wellington in Hackney, well-known in the 1970s for Irish drama. Cabaret and poetry readings are also sources of modern pub entertainment.

Another recent change has been the increasing number of pubs serving meals and coffee in addition to alcoholic drinks, which has turned them into informal kinds of restaurants. A parallel development has been the growth in wine bars and brasseries. As an alternative to going to the pub for a drink, people may now share a bottle of wine in their local wine bar. This continental influence is also reflected in other ways, such as in the organization of the Covent Garden Project, an area full of wine bars and open-air cafés, where the shops stay open late at night and all over the weekend, and street entertainment is always on offer.

While the popularity of wine bar and café culture has grown, the role of the cinema and theatre in Britain as a whole has shown a decline. Going to a film or a play has at least partly been replaced by watching television and video films at home, especially as the price of theatre and cinema tickets has risen sharply. In London this trend is rather less apparent, as both visitors and residents of the city still flock to the huge variety of films and plays that are premiered in the capital. Many of the theatres, built at the turn of the century, are worth visiting for their lavish decor alone, to see their ornate painted ceilings, chandeliers and plush velvet drapes. The Theatre Royal, Drury Lane, stands on London's oldest theatre site, the original one being built in 1663. The coloured neon lights of the West End shine brightly, and in Soho, the heart of theatreland, people bustle to and fro between clubs, cinemas, theatres, restaurants and bars. Yet outside the centre, local cinemas are gradually closing down and small theatres are struggling to stay alive.

Eating and drinking in the West End can prove quite expensive, but there are lots of other enjoyable ways of spending time, especially during the day, which are much more economical. Exploring some of the city's small, tree-lined squares, or strolling along the canal tow-path on a fine day is great fun in itself. Free bands play in the middle of Lincoln's Inn Fields at lunchtime; and organized walks pass through some of the interesting but lesser-known parts of the city such as the East End, not only the haunt of Jack the Ripper but also the centre for activities of 19th-Century Jewish Radicals. Spending the day at a museum, an art gallery, or getting a seat in the public gallery of the Law Courts is both fascinating and free. There are a host of things to do in London, whether you have a lot of money or not. For Londoners it is often the time that comes scarce, but however busy you are, making the time for leisure is always worthwhile.

Left: *A colourful display at the annual* Chelsea Flower Show, *held in the grounds of the Royal Hospital.*
Overleaf: *The bright neon lights of London's* West End *at night.*

RAYMOND
Showbar
La Vie en
ROSE
UNDERGROU
PAUL
RAYMOND
presents
moulin 1 2 3 4 5
Late Shows
EVERY NIGHT
NOW ONLY
£2:50
All Seats
One
Price
ENTERTAINMENT
ON THE
BIG
SCREEN
IN
COLOUR
NOW ONLY
£2:50
All Seats
One
Price
ADULT
RATED
MOVIES